ID0983030

THE FORBIDDEN POEMS

THE
FORBIDDEN
POEMS

BECKY BIRTHA

THE SEAL PRESS

Cover design and photograph by Clare Conrad

Library of Congress Cataloging-in-Publication Data
Birtha, Becky, 1948–
   The forbidden poems / by Becky Birtha.
     p.   cm.
   ISBN 1-878067-01-X
   I. Title.
PS3552.I7574F68   1990
811'.54--dc20   90-19836
                                 CIP

Printed in the United States of America
First printing, March 1991
10 9 8 7 6 5 4 3 2 1

Foreign Distribution:
In Canada: Raincoast Book Distribution, Vancouver, B.C.
In Great Britain and Europe: Airlift Book Company, London
In Australia: Stilone, N.S.W.

For My Friends

"I want to give them
everything: stories and poems
hugs, applause,
a voice to their melody. . . . "

Acknowledgements

This book was completed with the help of a Creative Writing Fellowship Grant from the National Endowment for the Arts, and with the support and encouragement of the Philadelphia Area Feminist Women Writers' Group.

"South Street" first appeared as a broadside published by the Binney & Ronaldson Press in 1984.

"In Response to Reading Children's Book Announcements in *Publishers Weekly*, February 12, 1982" First appeared in *Politics of the Heart: A Lesbian Parenting Anthology*, edited by Sandra Pollack and Jeanne Vaughn (Firebrand, 1987).

"Doors" first appeared in *Labyrinth*, July 1985.

"New Year's Eve, Race Street Meeting of Friends" and "Love Poem to Myself" both first appeared in *The Central Philadelphia Monthly Meeting Newsletter*, in March, 1987 and January, 1989.

"Plumstone" first appeared in *The South Street Star*, July 23, 1987, and also appeared in *By Word of Mouth: Lesbians Write the Erotic*, edited by Lee Fleming (Gynergy, 1989).

"Houseguest" first appeared in *The Evergreen Chronicles*, Summer, 1989.

"Black Women Writers' Conference" and "The Childless Woman Poems" both first appeared in *Common Lives/Lesbian Lives*, Spring, 1990 as "The Forbidden Poems."

"Assurances" first appeared in *With a Fly's Eye, Whale's Wit, and Woman's Heart: Animals and Women*, edited by Theresa Corrigan and Stephanie Hoppe (Cleis, 1989).

CONTENTS

CAST OF MANY COLORS

STAR CHILD

COUNTING MY LOSSES

DOORS

COMING TO TERMS WITH MYSELF

THE FORBIDDEN POEMS

CAST OF MANY COLORS

Cast of Many Colors

I flaunt my colors
        bright in my face
        intone them in
        traces my
        tongue retains
        my features full
        of my brownskin self
        these closecropped
        kinky curls
        all of me
        raw

I wear the labyris
        and little finger ring
        the double sign of venus
        dress in lavender
        the black the red the green
        wrap my head in fecund prints
        carry
        the kente cloth

I came by the strength of
        survivors,
        of west African, shanty Irish
        Catawba and Cherokee nations
        my given name a taken name
                rebirth
                birthroot
        taken for freedom times

I go by all my names
        third world
        black
        woman of color

sister/hermana
afroamericana la
negra la
lesbiana

I fasten the words across my heart
raise placards
carry banners
I raise
my voice and my
clenched fist lift
my eyes and I see
visions

I am the chosen one:
I have chosen to be myself.

South Street

I learned how to walk down South Street now
walk like I got some pride
take a long stride
let my hands swing free at my sides
lift my chin up high and keep my mind on
gettin where I'm goin.

And all them men hangin out on the corner by the bar
don't faze me none.
I look em dead
in the eye.
Be the first to speak—
Evenin.
Mornin.
Afternoon—
and walk on past.
They don't mess with me.

I take
up
some space and
cover
me some ground.
Y'all better look out, cause I
learned
how to walk down
South Street.

Vocabulary

Sat in English class and Mrs.
    Edith Osborne said
"There's a word for this what is it
    doesn't anybody know?"
I looked around
    the room full of
pale blank blinking faces
    and nobody did.

So I raised my hand and said
    "Poet's license."
Mrs. Edith Osborne said
    "What?"
I said
    "Poet's license?"
Mrs. Edith Osborne
    looked hard at me
and said real slow
    "No.
    That's wrong.
    It's called
    Poetic license."

Too bad I didn't know then
    to tell her what I know now:
Mrs. Edith Osborne,
    there's a word for this.
It's called
    Racism.

Mythology

You read us the words
you have written about
Demeter, Hecate, Diana.
When we no longer want to listen
you say—
But your people have myths of their own.
Why don't you find them out?
Why don't you write them down?
Why don't you bring them
for us to read?

Yes, we know that
our great great grandmothers
remembered many truths.
We also know
how those ancestors were
separated and sold
severed by the middle passage
disease, death
and design
so no two
women who spoke the same language
came to the same place.

To talk in the old tongues
was forbidden.
To learn to write
forbidden.
To sing the old stories
forbidden,

forbidden even
to speak secrets in
the sacred voice of the drum.

We live out our lives
in languages with no names
for the Goddesses
of our great grandmothers,
no characters in which to inscribe
their wisdom,
no verbs that encompass
their power,
no constructions that can contain
their rage.

Yes, we will find them out.
As we uncover and claim those words
we may never choose to write them down.
We will not be bringing them
to you.

Melanie

I lived with black folks all my life
hung out with the kids on my block
went to the neighborhood public schools
where all the tough kids went
showed up at church every Sunday
with the other little sisters

and they said
Girl—
You not black enough.
How come you talk like you white?
How come you read all them honky books?
How come you don't know how to dance the
Funky Broadway
can't party
can't boogie
can't really get down?
Child, what's the matter with you?
You dig? You
just ain't black enough.

So I went away to college
in Northampton, Massachusetts
where I found out
I was so black
they had to assign a Quaker to room with me
so black
no boy, white or black
would go out on a date with me
so black
that choosing to sit at my table in the dining room

was a definitive political statement
so black some people said
Can't she ever talk about anything else?
but most people
didn't hear me
didn't even see me
because
I was just too black.

How I Read Rilke

"Art too is only a way of living. . . . "
Rainer Maria Rilke, Letters to a Young Poet

upstairs at the co-op
I package dried fruit and nuts,
fresh cheese

work beside a woman who tells me
she is a writer, too
composer, music critic
she is older than I.
We search for talk to
touch a common space between us.

She winds from opera to Wagner
to German
poets—
we come to Rilke.

I start to tell her about the book,
describe how no work has
spoken to me that way
in seven years since,
but

she wants to know
how *I* read Rilke—
was it for a course in school?

I see
who
she sees

a young colored girl
in clean overalls

with hands that are
good at wrapping cheese.

I try to tell her
No
tell her
how I craved those letters
how I
waited for years
to be able to understand them
and then
how I read them again and again
tell her
how I *know*
he wrote that book
to give me
who I am.

Poem from a Clerk in the Law Library

Remove pages 601 to 602.
Insert pages 601 to 602.

To console myself, I make a list of
every story I've ever written in my life.

Remove pages 7,817 to 7,819.
Insert pages 7,817 to 7,822.

To console myself, I make a list of
every magazine that's ever published my work:
    Women, A Journal
    Women's Voices
    Womanspirit
    Womansmith. . . .
The editors must work at jobs like this one.
The magazines cannot pay.

Remove pages 60,000 to 60,000-2
Insert pages 60,000 to 60,000-2
To console myself, I make a list of
every black woman writer who has
ever written a book that I have
read— or even heard of.
The list goes on for twenty-seven pages.
Half of the women had to
publish the books themselves.

Remove pages 79,798.27A to 79,798.27Q.
Insert pages 79,798.27A to 79,798.27X.

To console myself I think about Zora Neale Hurston.
I think about her wealthy white employers.
I imagine the shock on that couple's
plump, complacent faces

when one of them picked up the copy of
the Saturday Evening Post
and discovered in it
a story
that was written
by their maid.

Class Consciousness

(for Sissy Rogers)

My Aunt Geraldine and Uncle Joey
fought out in the street one time.
A lot of nights, he didn't come home
and she went to her job
on second shift at the hospital
and left the kids alone.
The neighbors said they ran outside
with no clothes on, one winter
but that was about as bad as it got.

Nobody ever moved in
        with anyone else's wife
or had a baby by a different man
        from the one they were married to.
Nobody ever even
        got food stamps
        or AFDC
        until me.

I was about as bad as we got
smoked and drank and swore
loud enough for the neighbors to hear
tried every drug I heard about
dropped out of school
quit jobs for no reason
later, decided I was a lesbian
and told everyone.
I got arrested for hitch-hiking once but

Nobody ever
        shot anybody
Nobody ever
        went to jail

15

Nobody ever
        called the cops
        had to identify a body
        had to mop up blood off a floor

or anyway
nobody ever talked about it.

STAR CHILD

Women have come from Nigeria
Ghana, Senegal
Americas and islands, all
these women are authors
poets, scholars.
Downstairs in the hall
their bright books fill everyone's hands
spill across display tables
throughout the day
voices rising
articulate and strong.
They have read each other's work
can translate one another's
impassioned speeches on the spot
cite references and reviews. . . .
Nevertheless
in the dormitory after-hours
in the bathroom
side by side at the mirrors over the sink
the first friendly question
is always the same:
How many children do you have back home?

I

CHILDLESS WOMAN IN A PLAYGROUND

The children would let me be.
It is the mothers,
fathers who
stare at me.
Their bald curiosity
confronts across the box of sand
demands my justification.

There is no role for one like me
in this place.
I become a woman
who has lost her only child.
A daughter,
she would have been three this year.
I would have brought her here
to play with the others
in the sand.

The children's voices leap and fall
call to the fathers, the mothers.
It is my own child's voice
calling
crying
finally
pulling me away.

II

HABITS

This is the woman who turns
    saucepan handles inward on the stove,
    has done so for years
This is the woman who has memorized
    lullabies all her life
This is the woman who collects
    second-hand picture books,
    shelves them close to the floor
This is the woman who saves
    the prizes from cereal boxes,
    keeps a crate full of toys wherever she lives
This is the woman who places poisons and
    breakable objects high out of reach,
    leaves on a light in the hall
This is the woman who has
    no children in her life
This is the woman who waits
    until her lover goes to sleep
    before she cries

III

THE CHILDLESS WOMAN MEETS AN OLD FRIEND
    ON THE STREET

in the moment
when the baby turns
away from the stranger
to hide its face

in its mother's shoulder
I want
to be the mother
and not the stranger

IV

THE REST OF YOUR LIFE

Ask yourself
why you want this.
Who is it for?

The simple fact that you
carried her until she could walk
and even after,
that you consoled her
nursed her ills and
nurtured her well-being
delighted in her little hands and feet
her first few words
or that she hugs you freely
at three
is no guarantee
that at any time
in the rest of your life
you will be loved.

V

THIRTY-TWO

Sixteen and sixteen are thirty-two
old enough to be a grandmother now.
Among my people
in any other generation
I would not have had these choices.
The first Rebecca
raised on a slave plantation
bore nine children and
delivered ninety more
knitted socks
sewed dresses by hand from
feed sack prints
cooked over an open fireplace
chopped wood
butchered pigs
slaughtered chickens and
never learned to read.

The Stroller as an Instrument of
Female Torture and Oppression

In the Philippines they carry babies on their backs,
in China, Nigeria, Bolivia—all those
"underdeveloped" nations.
But here in Amerika, the acme of civilization,
we have strollers.

I should have suspected something
when that big box arrived from his mother:
elaborate deluxe model complete with
hand and foot brakes
rubber wheels with shock absorbers,
all stainless steel frame
webbed seat belt
sturdy canvas and vinyl seat
transparent plastic wind protector and
convertible fringed sun canopy.
Weighed five times as much as the baby.

After you spend three days on your hands and knees
with all your neighbor's tools
trying to read the directions which have been
poorly translated from the Japanese,
you have to solve the problem
of where to park the thing
in your one bedroom third floor apartment.
Then if you decide you want to use it
you have to figure out
how to get it down all those stairs
and—while you perform this Herculean feat—
what to do with the baby?
Put her in the stroller, and there's no way
you can move the thing down stairs.
But if you leave it sitting empty on the street
while you go back up for the baby
chances are excellent it'll be gone

when you return—
which might not be such a bad thing after all.

Once you hit the street with the baby in the stroller
forget about going downtown.
Forget about visiting anyone with steps.
Forget about riding the subway, the trolley, the bus
or even the escalator.
Forget about going through doorways into any
stores, banks, restaurants, office buildings
or laundromats.
Above all, forget revolving doors
or that turnstile thing they have in the supermarket.
About all you can do is stroll around the block
or through the park
and enjoy the envious smiles of other mothers
while the baby lounges complacently
in the shade
looking as if she expects to be waited on hand and foot
for the rest of her natural life.

The one and only time I took the baby
out in that thing
I made one stop— up on Fifty-Second Street
where an old lady had a table out on the sidewalk
selling African things.
I bought me something those brainy women ancestors
in Africa invented a thousand years ago,
even more efficient and functional
than the stroller.
It's called a piece of cloth.
It works.
You wrap the baby in it,
tie the ends around your middle
and go on about your business.

In Response to Reading Children's Book Announcements in Publishers Weekly, *February 12, 1982*

They say that children should have books
in which they can see themselves

    So I see they've got a line called
    "Baby's First Books":
    page after page of
    little fat smiling
    rosy-cheeked white babies

    And then they've got
    the "Mister" books:
    Mr. Happy
    Mr. Funny
    Mr. Strong.

    This week's picture books are starring
    Ferdinand Fox
    Roger, the cat boy
    and Honey Rabbit (also male).

    There is one happy family saga
    about a family of
    mice— no doubt complete with
    mother and sister
    all conveniently colored
    an inoffensive gray.

But our baby girl
loves books. We can't
keep her away from them.

    At the library on 52nd Street
    we pick up books about black kids
    and learn that black kids are mostly boys.
    At the branch on Rittenhouse Square

we discover books about
independent, capable little girls
who happen to be white.

Come to think of it
I never saw myself in any book
and I survived—
but that was thirty years ago.

We did find one book
(not in the library)
where one parent is black and the other white
like us
(of course,
they were of opposite sexes
still happily married
and both sets of grandparents were still speaking).

Downtown, there is
one gay bookstore
where we may not be able to
take the kid any more.
The government wants to
improve
our obscenity laws.

They can try, but
some things they can't deny.
Wherever she finds it
she'll piece together
some kind of identity—
figure it out
whatever way she can.
She's smart.
She'll put it together.

Portraits

I

Marian sends me snapshots of her children:
a little girl with a solemn stare
who's posed sideways, one hand
placed on the other,
a rugged gray-eyed boy with a laughing grin
and a toy clutched in his fist.

These children are bright, healthy
nourished and loved.
Their names are Scott Hubbard
and Judith Aurelia.
I keep them
like a secret
in a small white envelope
the size of a valentine.

II

In the mail I get circulars
from adoption agencies.
They are full of photographs
of children with special needs.
I study their faces carefully,
read every word.
It is not easy
to throw them away.

These children have been beaten
neglected, drug-abused.
These children are labeled
"serious medical risk,"

"severely delayed."
These children are disabled
disturbed, delinquent
depressed, discouraged
defeated

or black.

Star Child

(for Taisha)

You were four and a half your first Hallowe'en.
No one had ever shown you
    the stars
    the moon.
When I told you I would put
    the moon on your costume
you wanted to know how I would get it down.

I dressed you up to be Night
sewed you a satin cape
stitched on your own
    lemon velvet
    crescent moon.
I let you stick gold stars all over you.

Tonight you've gone home to your mother.
I never know when
    or if
    you'll come back.
But now you know the sky
    and celebrations,
you know that such things can be,
    in the world,
have words to call them by.

And I—
all over my house
    on the mirror
    inside my shoe
I'm still finding shiny stars sticking
    everywhere.

COUNTING MY LOSSES

I Gave It All Away for Being Loved

I'm lonely for who I used to be.
    Rubbing the cordovan polish
    into the straps of my shoes
the night before classes begin
I'm at home, alone
    with windows curtained
    against the night
radio turned on low:
    voice of some unknown woman
    singing the blues.

The tin slips
    from my stained fingers
    and clatters to the floor.
I'm caught
    in a sudden burst of tears.

That was me
    all those years
polishing shoes
darning, mending
ironing the soft collars crisp
getting ready
    for my life
to begin
    the next day
    the new season
me on the threshold
    of another year
    preparing

a fresh start
making ready
over and over again,
needing only
a point, a place to begin from
and waiting, awaiting
everything.

One Room at a Time

I

KITCHEN

The kitchen is neutral territory.
Sometimes we can both be here together
    with the lamp in the window lighted
    with supper in the oven
some nights
    this space is close and full
    the whole room warm and alive
and home.

First place in this house
    to feel like our own—
the walls are pine
door and window frames painted orange
cast iron frying pans hang in a line
    by size
    down the beam
    then the grater, collander, a spare
    basket, bunch of
    papery dried mint.
The teakettle shrills.

I would call it a truce
the way we spend hours here together
    some nights
drinking coffee
    chocolate, tea.

But there are no battles
    in this war
we don't fight

only talk

then silence
for long lapses of time.

II

STUDY

We withdraw to our separate rooms
at the top of the house

I stare for hours
out the window of mine—
    east—
at the facing side of another house:
    a wall of bricks,
at the peak of a church
    against the sky
tumbledown chimneys
the tops of
    renegade ragged ailanthus trees
    sprouted from back gardens
    zig-zag down the block
the broken fence of
    our own back garden
    littered and strewn
    unprotected
    in the reckless wind.

III

LIVING ROOM

Books, we said
make a room feel
    lived in.
But no one lives in this room.
The couch and chair face
    the ironwork doors of the firebox
    where there is never a fire.
We pass through
    quickly
    on our way between
    the kitchen
and other far parts of the house.

IV

FAMILY ROOM

We moved the sofa-bed up there and
    the rocking chair
put the sewing machine on a table
    under the window
    by the plants.

It'll be nice for guests, we said
    but we have none.

Cold drafts flow through this room
    whirl up the stairs and
    out at the top

slide in past the single layer of glass
    at the window
push down the chimney and
    through the holes in the fireplace screen.

The plants grow pale and spindly, then
    withered and dry.

V

BEDROOM

While we worked it was good.
We moved as a team
    tape, spackle and sand—
you painted, pounded nails,
I mitered corners with the coping saw.
Together we put up molding
    all around the top of the walls:
    mellow, dark-stained wood.

Thick brown carpet
and a curtain letting light
    through the door
the orchid posters—
now
this room is secure
square and safe
a cozy enclosure

and the bed
is a wide
no one's land

where we never kiss
each other deep and
long anymore
where
we are afraid and
no longer
make any
love
only
fall asleep
in one another's arms.

Expectations

sometimes it's worse than
    open fighting
the way nothing is special
    anymore

we don't decide to go out
    until the last minute
don't bother to get dressed up
    for each other

you don't want
    sex
and we agree
    to release that expectation

you still want
    to sleep with me, still
    hold me in your sleep
but I wonder for how much longer

in the morning you never
    reach for me
    or smile first
I get less and less
    from you

but keep trying
    to lower my ideals

and I want
    to stay with you
I want
    to feel loved
I want
    to go on giving
    whatever it takes
    from me.

Roses

By the time you return tomorrow
I'll be gone.
But this evening
I linger in the garden. It's rained.
The corner by the fence is full of roses.
I want to cut unopen buds for you
place them in a water jar
on the kitchen table.
They'd be full blown when you come in,
a surprise
a simple declaration:
      I thought about you.
      I cared about you.
      I wanted to make you happy—
a message in a language
you neither speak nor understand.

A Note of Thanks

with gratitude to Joan Larkin

coming back from Maine
coming in to Boston
from where I stayed last night at the house of a friend—
Porter Square Station, Cambridge. change trains.
loaded down with my backpack, sleeping bag,
the carryall with journal and notebook of poems
I follow the crowd down the steps to the red line
buy a token and trudge down more stairs—
the escalator doesn't work.
ahead of me
six more hours on the train today

I'm on my way home— but to what?
a desk in an office tomorrow morning
a lover who doesn't want me anymore
a summer that's over

at the foot of the stairs
the station is filled with
music!   bells,
opening petals of sound
woodwind threading through
a roundelay of strings—
something baroque
clear as springwater,
lapping around the quiet commuters,
falling and swelling through
this round arched, red tiled chamber

two women are making this music.
one has dark curls.
she plays two recorders

soprano and alto— at one time.
the other has a longer face, glasses.
she sits crosslegged and holds
a mallet in each hand, wrists supple and sure
she strikes the strings of a hammered dulcimer.
they are dressed like me in plain, simple clothes.
if I lived in this city, perhaps they would be my friends

I give them a dollar of my change
place it in the open case that is littered with bills and coins.
the woman playing the dulcimer nods at me.
I want to give them
everything: stories and poems
hugs, applause,
a voice to their melody— miss my train,
stay, and listen out the morning

but the station stuffs with noise.
I cross the threshold.
after the doors slide shut
the darkhaired woman turns
and sees me through the glass
and smiles.
I hear their melody
long after Porter Square Station

on the train
a black woman a generation
older than I, with gray in her knotted hair
sees my bags
and my tears
and crosses the car
to ask me why I am crying.
I tell her it was the music

but just as likely it was
the women who might have been lovers
it was Maine, the summer ending
the kicking around New England by myself
the coming home—   whatever
I wanted to answer her— it was
something I could not tell

On Being Stood Up at the Ticket Window at Suburban Station, 16th and Kennedy Boulevard, Philadelphia, PA

If I had thought I was going to spend
an hour and fifteen minutes in a train station
underground
I would have planned it differently.
I would have brought my knitting
a good novel
or at least a better pen
and a decent notebook— something besides
the empty spaces on this train schedule.

I want my hour back. I want back
my dollar that I fed into the phones
because of you:
25¢ for a phone that didn't work
25¢ to talk to your answering machine
a quarter to call your lover's collective house
where you hadn't been seen all day
and another to reach the people who were expecting us
for the potluck dinner later this afternoon.

If I'd known you weren't going to show
I would have planned the whole day differently
gone to that party after all
or spent the time outside working in my garden
I could have sat in a lawn chair in the back
yard for an hour drinking iced tea. It was
only an hour we'd have had
together, anyway
before the dinner began.
Was that too much to ask from your
complicated life?

Yes, I am finally angry at you.
All around me other people are
cheery and punctual

meeting their friends
buying their tickets
catching their trains.
And here I sit, on a bench, with three other losers
smelling pizza
listening to Muzak
and keeping my eye on the ticket window
while the contents of my covered dish
loses its chill and seeps
through the brown paper bag.

Don't think I never got here.
Don't think I went home.
Don't think I'll forget
this happened.
Sooner or later,
you're going to have to deal with this.

Poem for Flight

There will come a day—
it is not far off now—
when you wake in the morning and know
you were meant to be happy
and that you want it
more than you want
things, or memories
any concrete place called home
all the strings of the past that fasten you,
more than you want
justice or pride:
your old clay image of yourself
or the faint chance
that all that has gone wrong
may still change.

It is you who hold
the power to change.

And whatever it is that holds you
whatever it is you think you cannot live without
the time has come to open your hands and
let it go.
Run
flee
disappear
break loose
take wing

fly by night
move like a meteor
be gone.

If you fear it will never be possible
think of Harriet
who traveled alone
the first time
who finally freed three hundred people
but first
had to free
herself.

Ambulatory

Six weeks later
the cast is cut off
then one by one
the crutches laid aside.
My life seems possible again,
my left leg encased
in a heavy steel brace
that feels like freedom.

I can pick the kale in my garden
I can carry it in my hands.
I can go out alone
I can take the bus
I can be on my own.
I can walk.
I can walk
I can walk away.

Primary Passion

The kittens nurse
their mouths greedy
their bodies
nose to tail tip
trembling with desire
bumping and butting
squirming atop one another
rooting through damp, mottled fur
frantic to reach that
fulfillment
for which there are no words.

> I wanted passion too,
> to be craved and sought after
> hungered and thirsted for.
> I didn't perceive the
> danger in desperation,
> that insatiable mouth always
> wanting, draining me down.

My friends, two women lovers
bring their two-year old
and take their pick of the litter:
the gray, the fat, full friendly one
who doesn't shy away
from Kaitlin's greedy touch.
Linda tucks it inside her coat
and says, "I'm sorry, little one
there's no way
for you to say goodbye to your family,
but now you're coming home."

> Not long ago, I fell asleep
> in my own bed
> and didn't know

I'd wake up understanding
I couldn't live anymore
in the same house
estranged
your desire dead and my
anger grown to a
monstrous, mouthing
passion to
consume me.

The four remaining kittens
black, white, tortoise shell
and gray calico
nurse again tonight.
Have they noticed that
someone is missing?
I want to tell them
drink deep, drink well
this night let your quivering passion
be all there is.

Once, on a night I no longer remember
we made love with each other
deeper than milk, than blood
with that wild instinctive intensity
for which there were never words—
the same way we had
loved one another
a hundred times before.
How could either of us know
we never would again?

From Here On In

There is a meadow set deep in a wood
like a stone in a ring.
There is a meadow set deep in a wood
like an eye in a storm.
There is a meadow set deep in a wood
like a lover's sweet secret center.
Two women are making love in the meadow.

One of the women lies on her back
her arm bent across her face.
She is wearing a white dress, deep in ruffles
The sash trails out to the side across the grass.
The other woman comes up by her head
bends down to lift her arm aside
and begins to kiss her face. . . .

I fill in all the details until I come
then emerge in a burst of
sobbing.

For years I wouldn't let myself
do this.
I allowed my mind to imagine
only you.
And not very often.

You said the way I loved myself
kept me from loving you.
You thought the way I loved myself
took something away that should be yours
little enough as there is of love.

And I loved you more than anything! I remember
waking you with my tongue
waking you with my fingers trailing

across your breast
pressing my face into the lap of your skirt
when you came in from work
I could sleep the whole night
holding you.

Now I'm holding my own.
I plot
the course of this venture alone.
Follow the way through the wood
and I know this wood
follow the trail to the meadow
know every twist and drop and rise
follow the path to the center
I know my way home.

This gift no one can give you:
feeling loved.
This is a gift I have to give
myself.

How to Be Alone

After ten years I am learning
how to be alone again.
Sometimes it's easy.
In a whispering rain
I carry my belongings
as far into the woods as I can find a path
pitch my blue tent
beneath a thorn tree
and for three days call it home.

I am learning how to be alone again.
Sometimes it's awesome.
There are seven hundred women here
their tents ring the round field
with peaks and domes
all sizes, all shapes, all colors
the women fill the hall
where meals are served
their seven hundred voices too loud to hear.
I gird myself
to enter.

I go to the concert alone, slip in late
in the dark
it is easy
even in the crowded room
to find a seat for one
but I can't laugh at the comedienne
I don't know this music
the claps and cheers grow
distant behind my back.
Already I can find my way without a light
miss the puddle
spot the crooked overhanging branch of pine
see how the sky breaks through the trees

above the clearing.
I crawl through the flaps
to pull on another layer
and embark again.

At the juncture of trails, this time
I walk the way
I haven't been before
my flashlight in my pocket:
there is nothing I am afraid of here.
The road climbs high to a
second meadow.
When I reach the crest
the sky is filled with lights
the thickets so full of voices
it's awesome
cricket and katydid, locust and toad
call and answer one another
and I'm safe—
in this crowd
in this long, loud humming song
that carries through
the night.

In Season

So this is how it is, then,
to come to the other end
of being loved.
I flip the pages of my
old journals
sift the years in my mind
keep searching for
the reason: the mistake.

    I loved.
    I did no better
    no worse than others.
    I changed in many ways
    but there were those ways
    I could not change.

        In my garden
        dying is continual.
        Red petals fall from a full blown rose.
        The spider snares a candlefly.
        Impatiens do not return the following spring.

But we who live in houses try
to prolong the life of everything
with endless probing, speculation
the posthumous examination
as though death could be explained, prevented
as though,
without illness or injury
life might last infinitely. No.

        Something is born and grows
        lovely
        is loved
        changes

reaches the end of its time
and dies.

> In my garden
> bleeding hearts
> winter over.
> Sweet alyssum
> reseeds itself.

Poem for the Loss of the Relationship

Someone has given you a rare antique
pottery bowl
hand-crafted by a highly skilled artisan
long ago.
Its shape and its color delight you.
You love the feel of it in your hands,
its thickness and weight.
It is one of a kind—
no other exactly like it exists in the world.
You want to take excellent care of it
to appreciate it every day
to keep it forever.

As the years go by you grow
increasingly interested in ancient pottery
for the sake of this single vessel.
You begin to read voraciously,
learn to identify different styles and periods
types of glazes and clay.
You attend lectures at universities,
showings at museums. You become
a resource to others.
Your life revolves around this work
and you love it.
The exquisite hand-crafted bowl remains
most precious to you in all the world.

One morning when you pick up the bowl
it slips from your fingers
and tumbles to the concrete floor
where it smashes into a thousand pieces.

Poem for the Loss of My House

I keep thinking about my grandparents
how, in the Depression, they rented out rooms
and then, the whole second and third floors
of the house on Monticello Street.
And the family crowded into the first floor
all four kids
and they lived that way
through those long, lean years
when my father delivered newspapers every morning
and stood in bread lines at the end of the day
and my grandmother cooked beans
a different way every night
but the bank foreclosed in the end
and they lost the house anyway.
My grandfather was so bitter
he said he would never own another house.
But one day he did.

Poem for the Loss of the Garden

Time of trouble
time of losses:
my love
my home
and now I've given away
my garden—
to a carefully chosen friend
who's already planted
even green rows
and left the corner chives
to bloom.

I wander in
someone else's garden
past someone else's white birch
touch her shiny moonpaper bark
like wet silk.
I'll pick someone else's buttercups
for a jar on my morning table
wild mustard
may apple
tulip tree
oh, I know
you all.

In someone else's garden
I lean to smell the irises
one after another
along the wooden fence
each a fragrant crown of color—

lilac
lavender
royal purple
take me home.

Now something white-tailed and winging
lifts from the green,
wing-spread wide
soars under the vine-thatched trellis
through the open gateway
and straight to the heart.

Poem for Protection in the Wake of Love

Lapping the rocky shore, the tide's going out
leaving a crust of pebbles and periwinkle shells
mussel cups, pearl lined, each filled to the brim
with clear sea water and sky.
If I were a creature now, I know I'd be a shellfish
spun into a round, brown spiral
sunk in the twilight marsh where the cove's lip
brushes the sea, I'd be
on my own
wherever the waves may have left me—
home.

Counting My Losses

If I begin with the crocuses
snowdrops, then clusters of yellow
daffodils against the wooden fence
heavy-scented hyacinth and bleeding heart
each in the order that it appears
year after year—

if I begin again and stop
and cry for every open-throated crocus,
how many days
weeks   seasons   years
before I'd reach the hollyhocks—
the last of all I planted there?

If I could reach the hollyhocks
I would be halfway through
one summer
but I gave ten years of my life to this
and how many summers
until I recover?

Perennial.
I though that meant predictable
dependable, lasting
what you can come to count on
year after year anew,
what you've planted being returned to you.

In this garden I grew flowers
and what never flowered:
the lilac sapling a yard high,

a gift from my mother I had to leave behind
and wisteria I started
earliest of all

knowing how long it would take to spill
those first loose falls of lavender.
Counting my losses,
is this where I begin?
Or end—
three more years to first flowering—

I couldn't stay.

DOORS

Doors

The carpenter came
this week.
She finished the two small jobs
we had asked of her.
She told me the solid wooden door
I had found on the street
for my room
would fit just fine—
and it did.

Downstairs
she took the back door
from its hinges
planed the edges and
aligned it right,
hung it plumb
so the bolts slide
into the strike plate,
flush.
Now the lock turns
easily.

I can go out to the garden, now.
Sweet smelling curls of wood
have fallen among the purple violets.
I can close the door to my room
lie in the patch of east sun
that laps across the floor.

And I wonder,
that I never thought how all the while

what I needed was so simply
this:
a door, to the outside
that opens
a door, to the inside
that shuts.

The Full Moon Rising in a Country Town

I walk in the last of the light
follow the winding village streets
valleyed by soft shoulders of grass.

People live here.
They paint their steep-roofed houses white.
I pass a baby's swing on a porch,
a fortress of firewood
heaped high as the oaken eaves.

A lone house faces an open field.

At the end of the street
the moon lifts out of a meadow—
pale bright pumpkin globe

I want to live here, too
want for
mine a room at the top of the house
mine, the moon in the window
this close, cloudful sky
lilac, violet.

Creation Dream

Many women
writers gathered
in a distant place
to learn from one another.

On the last day
I found something growing in vines on a wall.
I didn't know what it was.
I didn't know whether it was plant or animal
or a new thing come into the world
       that no one had yet discovered.

I wanted to carry it with me.
I lifted it gently from its place
       cradled in my two hands.

It was like something a spider had spun.
It was blue and luminous
       with many soft, bulgy folds.
Perhaps it was a flower
       or sea creature
       a mushroom
       a heart.
In the center of its body
       there was a single eye.
It appeared to be smiling.

Thumbprint Dream

We are traveling again—
day's end in a distant town. I go
for a walk away from you
to watch the sky.
My hand slips into my pocket—
among assorted objects feels
a small, smooth stone.
I draw it out.

Milky, translucent
it is no bigger than
the end of my thumb.
Red lines are etched across
and down one surface
to form a grid in the center.
The oval of the other side
is marked with a thumbprint,
also red.
I know it is mine.

I return wanting to show you the stone.
I empty my pockets, purses
find things we've been missing for days
and weeks—
but no small stone.

I try to describe what I found.
You lose interest
anxious to sleep,

to be on the road by early morning.
You say it doesn't matter

and it's true.
I have the stone.
I know it.

Visitant

A woman has entered my house
though all the doors were locked last night.
She is no one I know.
Ancient and wrinkled
wrapped in many layers
she could be mistaken on a street corner.
She is neither dirty nor crazy.
Almost immediately
I know she is a witch
and know I'm safe.

She asks for paper.
I take up the lined tablet
where I labored with a purple pen
on many pages,
where I have drawn figures and diagrams
trying to solve my problem.
I tear off layer after layer
to reach the blank sheets beneath,
hand her the pad—
she stuffs it into her pocket.

I remember to offer to hang her wraps.
She accepts.
We move to stand in the door of the closet.
She hands me layer after layer
of clothing:
her hooded cape
loosely handwoven of soft colored wools,
a black jacket and vest

richly embroidered in gold.
With every layer removed she becomes
younger and more beautiful—
though her face is plain—
until she's a maid in a pale cotton shift
with short-cropped hair, light eyes, and is
younger than I.

She invites me to
line the pockets
of her outer garments
with food.
It will help, she says, turning
toward the kitchen, the table.
I bring bread to fill the many openings
while she works easily
at my trouble.
In only seconds, it seems, she has left me
    an answer
    resolution
    a destiny

    gifts:
words on paper.

Toad House

I love even the weeds in this
scant hundred square feet.
I call them by their names:
white snakeroot, smartweed
lambsquarters, sourgrass—
I let them live.

In spring
every week I treat myself
to a six-pack of annuals:
lobelia, sweet William, ageratum
survive exhaust fumes
from passing cars,
survive the city water
survive the polluted air.

But this evening I found
something I surely never planted here:
a spotted brown and
yellow mottled toad.
Where did it come from? Leslie asks,
The parking lot next door?

I say the Goddess sent it.
I say it's a blessing, a sign.
I say it means I must be doing
something right
this summer
and hastily repot a houseplant
to knock a small rounded door
in the empty clay container.

Turned upside down among
the California poppies,
it's ready. Closeby,

I fill a flat enamel pan with water
and push it under the Wisteria vine—
a toad bath and fountain.
I hope it looks like home.

At twilight, when traffic slows
when construction crews have emptied
the building site across the street
when the lightning bugs come out,
I go into the garden
and speak softly to this small
kindred
creature:

I know who you are.
I invite you to stay.

Assurances

A blessing has come to this garden:
Four black and yellow spiders
spin their webs from vine to corner
petunia to geranium, and hang still
through the long hot days, waiting for food.
I make myself
simple meals from garden vegetables
eat with my chopsticks from the painted bowl.
I'm waiting too: word from you.
An answer. An ending. Your decision to
no longer share this life with me—
if a life can be shared!
The spiders' webs are complex,
intricate like handmade lace
symmetrical and open as windows.
Each is perfect and complete, each
is all it needs to be.
The spiders never speak
to one another, or visit, yet I know
each one is aware that the other three
share this same garden. And aware of me.
There's some way that
I'm connected, some sheer strand
that, by all logic, ought to break
when an obstacle slams into it,
or human hand, but holds.
The spider falls, plummets
carefully to safety and patiently
climbs to mend the web
to begin again.

The Healing Poem

There is a healing power in the sky.
For times when you cannot weep—
travel on foot
a morning's measure; find
a vast unbounded field of sky
then, spend the whole of a day
beneath it.
In your house
keep one window free
panes shining full with blue or gray—
you must never stray far
from the sky.

There is a healing power in the land.
When what you would change
you cannot change,
take tool to hand and
work the earth:
spade deep and turn it over,
let it crumble, sift out every stone.
Near your home,
set off a stretch of ground;
feed it, keep it
growing.
If you must leave the land,
do not leave for long.

There is a healing power in you
when reason fails—
you cannot overcome the problem
with your mind.
It is in your fingers
that lace and mend
in the bend of your back when you
swing the axe,

shovel coal or snow.
It is in your voice
singing, released
when your feet pick up
the pound of a beat, leap and whirl—
turn full around:
return to yourself.
Do not forget to
keep your powers alive.

The healing is in these words—
When you want very much
something you cannot have
you must begin again

A Deeper Healing

This is a healing poem
for when you cannot dance
and cannot work
and cannot walk.
Concentrate on
the things you still can do.
       Breathe.
       Dream.
       Love.
       Change.

Accept It Gracefully

When you want very much
something that you *can* have
consider it a gift;
accept it gracefully.

Six Days in Oregon

Midnight in Oregon. I'm wide awake
alone in a state where I know almost no one
alone in my life again. This morning
I followed a lumber trail through a wood
and into a meadow of felled trees. I found
a green pinecone like the ones I used to find
down by Cresheim Creek when I was a child.
I found the way these tall pines begin:
tiny seedlings less than an inch in height
light colored as lichens, and the ground as thick
with them as moss— that grow to these spires of trees
hundreds of feet in the sky. I could see now
all around the circle— I was in
a community of trees.

           Tonight I lead
three others into the clearing, where we find
a community of stars— the Milky Way. We stay
and talk of different cities in the dark.
All four of us see the meteor that streaks
a trail down the slope of the sky. And someone asks
me if I have a lover in that city
I left at the other end of the continent.
I know the answer now. In these six days
in Oregon, I have learned: that I know what I want;
that I had forgotten how many stars there are;
that my life is open at one end. I have learned
I could come back here. I could find the way. And that
I can leave from here for anywhere in the world.

New Year's Eve,
  Race Street Meeting of Friends

Imagine! You are traveling along
on the journey through your life.
It's a winter night
in the heart of a great city
when you come to an immense brick building
where you expected to make a stop
but the windows are all dark, and the doors locked.
Still, you notice that there is a light within
and, yes. One door has been left open
for you. Once inside, you see that more light
comes from somewhere above, and you climb stairs
and at the top of the staircase find
a large bright empty room
where a fire has been laid and lit
and is burning effortlessly,
where bread and cakes are arranged on a table
and a circle of comfortable chairs
is drawn up around the fire. You take a seat
and fall into grateful silence.
Then, one by one
others come into the room, smile at you,
seat themselves before the fire, too,
and take up your silence.
And all of them are friends!

Driving Across the Continent

The essence is this:
I was twenty.
I had left home.
I was on my way across the country
with a knapsack, a sleeping bag,
a stranger.
My money was nearly gone.
We were far out west.
The time was early in the new year,
winter, sunrise.
Sky like nothing I had ever seen
was everywhere.

There was not another car on the road.
The road was climbing,
twisting and climbing
to the top of the canyon
where suddenly, around a bend
another vehicle loomed, lurched close
and passed us on the narrow road—
a yellow schoolbus full of
silent Navajo children
their solemn eyes gazing past the windows
at the wide, familiar face
of the ageless land.

I WANT MORE FROM YOU THAN WORDS

Victoriana

Lodging's
a nineteenth century guest house
in this seaside town.
In the Victorian bedroom
there is a marble topped chest;
pale towels grace the corner washstand,
wall paper a diminutive floral print
flocked pink.

In the high four-posted bed
you are asleep
stripped clean of your layers of dressing.
You said
you don't care
for all this ruffle-edged
elegance.

But the light
through the handstitched piecework quilt
glows
across your body
pink as the inside chambers
of a deep sea shell.
Your hair, against the eyelet pillowcase
matches the headboard's
chestnut gleam.

Your face
from the sun all yesterday
is ripe and fresh,
open in sleep this morning
as the blossoming roses
across the trellis
downstairs
at the garden gate.

Parting Ways

After we've said goodbye
this time
you lean against the bricks
of the station wall.
I watch through the tinted glass:
white bib overalls
pale blue workshirt laundered fresh
the red kerchief folded wide and
tied, in a band
across your brow
your face flooded with shining tears

You told me: last year
you cried in the train
half the way home
cried through New England country towns
through customs and
changing trains in Canada, cried
far into Ontario

Hands hang at your sides
eyes keep returning to me
your eyes are full
your face
upturned and open—
my hands wind tight in my lap
I force my shaky smile
through the glass to you.
I keep my place.

I long to be beside you
out of Montreal in the morning

beside you on that train
I would know what it is
I want
to say—
tell who you are to me, who
we are to each other—
I want to cry
with you
and hold you
all the way from
Montreal to Toronto
Toronto to Kingston
Kingston to Ingersoll

I keep my place.
The coach pulls away
space between us springs and grows—
I am going home.
I am going home to someone.
I am going home to someone I love.

I Want More From You Than Words

Thanksgiving: newly friends
we walk a mile or two into the woods.
We are close enough to touch
but there is so much space here—
the trail climbing high
above the creek—
we pace ourselves
side by side along the gravel roadbed
in the little that's left to this day.
I want more.

We never stop
talking the whole time
trying to learn each other's lives:
Who we spent this day with
in other years
talk of old lovers, what went wrong
talk of our time alone—
I have more for you than stories.

It begins to rain
but we stay on in the gray mist
walking.
Who else would walk so
long in the rain
but lovers?
I lend you my kerchief.
You knot it behind your neck,
a spot of bright red color
in the stark, leafless wood.
I know you'll keep it

as if by accident,
wear it when I'm not with you—
and I want to give you more.

Now we've turned homeward
it's all a downhill sweep—
already we've reached a bridge
you don't remember
crossing.
It's nearly night
the light gone
gray, this brief
day too quickly closing.

So late in season
after so long a time untouched
under this overcoat of
old pain,
passion awakens slowly
but does awaken.
There's rain on your face
crimson in your cheeks
steam lifts from your parted lips.
Moisture clings to our clothing
seeps against skin.
Behind you the trees drip,
their black bark saturated.

Down the vortex of the valley:
the pull of the black water
riverward—

I've a river, rising
coursing its current
swift and strong
through the core of me
and I want—

I want
more from you
than words.

Storms

Unexpected passion
sweeps through my life
I can't pretend that nothing is wrong.
Shaking, my voice breaking into sobs
I have to excuse myself from groups
and when friends ask how I have been,
I lie, but my eyes fill with tears.
I no longer keep promises
have no control
I say I am falling to pieces.

You tell me you call these times storms.
They occur in your life, too.

You are the storm in my life—
unpredicted. Overwhelming.

Electricity cracks, charges the air
the sky split with sudden searing
illumination
I hear the scattered drops gather
to one incessant sounding
Open to let the gale drive through me
let the water stream my upturned face
Smell the earth soaked full
slaked and satiated
with clean, hard rain.

I will not think of destruction
that lies in a storm's wake.

As though I have no choices
I let you happen.

There Is No Other Way to Read Them

(for the poet Laurie J. Hoskin)

They are like a map of the sky
these poems
a map of the sky at night,
perfect bright points of light
against paper blue.
Lines connect to
draw them into clusters.
Images appear.

And your life is like
the real
sky at night.
Who *are* all these
constellations?
I cannot tell
where one ends and another
begins
the sky is as full as an ocean
the sky is overpopulated
the sky is a crowd
no map
will ever guide me through.

These poems are a blueprint,
a chart
with no terrestrial counterpart.
I leave notes to myself
between the pages—
Try this one again.
Start on page 47
tomorrow night—
and read them as if they all
all of them
were written for me.

Intimate Friends

The night Kathy offered
a lift into town
as far as Broad and Vine
we both agreed
though it was another five blocks
for you, eleven for me
but we could keep talking
walking side by side
down Broad Street
barelegged in our summer clothes
at ten o'clock on a weekday night.

All we ever do together is walk
and talk at twilight,
stopping at every garden
in the neighborhood.
We take a long time on
my front porch, or yours
saying goodbye
in the humid hush of summer night
until one of us offers to
walk the other home
so we can talk a little longer.

Then we spend the whole of a day together
under the sky.
The path becomes a steep, uphill climb.
At the peak, I take a chance and tell you
what I feel.
Next day I find
a letter in my door that says

you can't accept
a kind of love that you cannot return.
We agree to be intimate
friends.

You go away for a week.
I imagine you in the country
in the sun, writing poems
your garments patches of
turquoise and magenta
brighter than any garden.
When you come home
you tell me about the grasses
that filled the fields with red
their tops
a waving undulation.

Now it's my turn to be away
far in the Northwest where
I keep you on my mind.
In the meadow I count
seven kinds of grasses
without moving from one spot.
In a letter I write
I miss you
wondering
if that's too much
to say.

What the Sculpture Said

I

Home from the lesbian weekend
I brought a piece of sculpture
a Myriam Fougère
a pair of tiny
terra-cotta lovers
embracing
brown limbs entwined
their ripe, full breasted bodies each
other's enclosure

I wrapped it in brown ribbon,
caught you aside a minute before a meeting.
I gave it embarrassed, worried
I'd picked the wrong time
it had cost too much
you wouldn't want it
it was too explicit when
I wanted it to be art for you

I wanted it to say everything
I couldn't,
with ease and eloquence—
the figures not me and you but
you and your lover—
that I accepted her
and you as two.

You took it, surprised, then
uncomfortable. You
saw a different message:

Passion. Desire
raw clay-naked and
burn-colored fired hard
in your open palm.
You showed it to your lover. She
wanted you to give it back.

Tonight you tell me this and
I don't know what to
hide, where to turn
my feelings, how to see you
any other way
how to stop
these words I can't tell you,
so have come bearing
gifts again:

a glossy ripe eggplant
cut from my garden yesterday.
It sits where you've
planted it, by a book with a
beige cloth cover
under a lamp. It looks
like a solemn sculpture
a still life
simple as a rose in a crystal vase
it could grace your table a day or two
squat and purple and
plain. Ostensibly
innocent.

What the Sculpture Said

II

The Lovers:

Yes, we are a tangle of passion
pure and unrefined.
We have survived
the fire.
We are no easy message to take.
We insist upon your full attention.
We speak to you with one mouth.
You respond with your body.
We claim you.

The Eggplant:

I am plain and dark.
I am smooth to the touch
ripe and round-bellied as a
drum.
I am infintely patient.
I have spent my whole life
growing slowly ready
in the sun.
I am in your house.
I am on your table.
You will not think twice about it—
before you know it you will have
consumed me.
I will be you.
I am full of my own seed.

Wanting

You're in blue when I say good-bye:
    round-yoke smocked, bare shouldered
    two of us summer-skirted on the porch step in the sun
    at the house where you no longer live, but you
    don't even ask how I knew to come here this morning
to find you.

I show you the trade beads I strung long ago
    that I know I need to carry with me
    this week that I'll be away
I say they're for wanting what I can't have.
    You finger every one
    and give me your pocket handkerchief to wrap them in.
There's a mockingbird only a yard away
    calling her cry of alarm
    but we're all smiles for each other this sunshiney morning.

Seven days later when I come home I want to come home to you.
    I'm at your door at dusk, you in the same blue
    and I'm in it too, tonight, up-ruffled at my shoulders
You offer me melon and blueberries, lemon-grass tea
    sit far across the room from me
    in this unfamiliar place you've moved to. You
play music that makes me cry
    and tell me you've become lovers
    with someone else.

You give me
    the dry fruit of the sweetgum tree
    full of spikey points in all directions
    and holes, like a hundred baby bird beaks
    open,
    wanting.

Houseguest

You've invited yourself
to stay over—
you have business in my neighborhood
the following morning.

I invite you
to sleep
alone on the single futon in my study
or, alone on the double in my room
if you want more space

Or— I say, in a small voice,
not looking at you—
You can sleep with me.
A throwaway line.

You choose solo,
the narrowest of beds.
It's sleep you want.

And I wake warm in the brightest of mornings
knowing I'm free
to want what I want—
and to accept what's given,
realizing I can change
my expectations

savoring the gift of a friend asleep
in a spare room with an open door
just at the other end
of the passageway.

THE WAY I WANT TO BE FRIENDS

She Who Makes Me Feel Welcome in My Own Home

My friend comes to stay
the night with me.

I cut ripe roses for the kitchen table
put pinks and marigolds
in a vase on the bathroom sink.

I shred sweet garden lettuce
and the last of the spinach
to make a meal for us,
fill a glass pitcher with cold tea
and a spray of mint.

I choose the china plates,
cloth napkins
rather than paper.

It is easy for me to do these things
for my friend.
They give me pleasure.

She notices every detail,
tells me how much she likes each one.

We eat at the garden table:
a wide slab of gray slate.
We are up until all hours
talking.

I spoon out camomile blossoms
and brew her a cup of pungent tea.

When we finally get ready for sleep
I pull out clean, deep blue sheets

for her bed,
fresh towels for the morning.

She says she feels very cared for.

And it's easy,
so easy for me to do this.
It gives me so much pleasure.

In the morning
I slice strawberries into the
homemade yogurt.
I make her coffee,
butter the bread before
toasting it.

I walk her to her train
listening, and telling
all the while.

And she makes it easy
so easy for me
to believe in
my ability to love.

Abundance

Just off the Nightowl
arriving half an hour late
from Baltimore, Maryland—
quarter to two in the morning—
I stumble down the platform into your embrace.

You're wide awake, bright-eyed and cheerful
leading the way across vast stretches of marble
past winged statues and fifty-foot columns
threading us through the majestic grandeur
of this colossal monument
where you must have been the only one
waiting to meet the train.

You told me you're this nice to all your friends, but
what an array of presents!
A glass of orange juice capped with a colorful lid,
the season's last luscious
gold-flecked plum.

Out to the parking lot—
the air snaps cold.
Your back seat's filled:
fresh broccoli and sweet red peppers
from the Amish farmer's stall,
a head of cauliflower
creamy and perfect

as a wedding bouquet.
How could you already know
so well what I love

most of all
maple leaves, red-stemmed and veined
their gold suffused with glowing
like the essence of this season
like what ripens inside me.

Carioca

The summer you and I were friends we lived
in collective houses a few blocks apart
deep in the thick of the city. We both slept
outside that summer, on the roofs of our
respective homes.
                    This I remember:
                    One night
I bought two carioca ice cream cones
and carried them to your door. Your housemates said
you'd already gone to sleep. I carried them
through the house, three stairwells up, and up
a ladder through a trapdoor to the roof
where you lay under a quilt, under stars
deep in the thick of night. I surprised you
my two hands filled, bearing those dense rich globes
heavy laden with thick, sweet melting cream
both of us wide awake now and laughing
under the stars.
                    Then I gave
                    yours to you.

The Dancers

I visit for an hour
at the end of a crowded day

you give me two shells from your stay
at the beach—they are totally unalike

one hovers, a cave with a small safe window
one's wingbone open, an arch, a bridge

head to head
they are having a conversation

I line them up along the margin of your journal
now they are in a dance class getting ready

to go across the floor
the round one moves off in a sure, steady push

the other would rather improvise
they have very different body types, you say

yes, but they're intimate friends
now they are resting quietly while we two talk

I walk home in a sure, steady push
that makes me safe

I carry a shell held in each closed hand
weightless, balanced

All I Remember

Wheeled up from recovery
out of the elevator
flat on a green-sheeted gurney
all I remember is
how happy I was to see my friends
one after another
down the hall
their faces
leaning over me
in smiles
their hands taking hold
of my own
my friends
moving beside me
to a door
where more of them clustered
in a room that
turned out to be mine.
All I remember is
talking and telling them everything
but mostly
how much it meant that they
came there
to me—
I didn't know what I looked like.
I didn't know I sounded delirious.
I didn't know I was crying.

Scraps

i.   chocolates,
notecards.
everyone wishing me
well again.
a blue ribbon
fallen from some
thin paper
twisting narrow
through my fingers

ii.   window ledge—
city a mere
backdrop for this
display of flowers:
Carla's freesia
Sandy's crimson
chrysanthemums in the
Perrier bottle
next to
extravagant
abundance from my
co-workers—
parade ends with
big, thick-stem
open-face
sunflower could
only be from
Mary's garden

iii.   dizzy
spacey
heady
giddy
but content.
perplexed,

I don't know
where the pain's gone,
don't connect this with
the morphine
until someone asks me—
stoned?

iv.   night nurse
stops behind the curtain
before entering
reads my chart—
torn tendon
orthopedic surgery
more medication—
she's surprised when
I remember
from last night
and call her
Rose

v.   awake at midnight
it's all right
if I
can't sleep can
slip on the headset
Sara lent me
turn on
Saturday night
my favorite my
downhome
delta blues

vi.   I'd stay
another night

if they'd
let me,
even longer—
tended and tucked
between crisp, flat
white,
wrapped in
gifts and
goodness
handled with
care, this
feels like
what Laura always
wishes me—
safe home.

Total Dependency on the Lesbian Community

I never knew there were so many ways to
make a cup of tea—
with caffeine or without?
with sugar
with honey
with lemon
with Realemon
with lemon that doesn't even pretend to be real
not hot enough, and growing colder by the minute
while waiting for the toast
too weak, or already
too strong when it arrives
but with no place to put the sodden tea bag
(we're not even dealing on the level of loose leaves
teaballs and strainers and other
implements of destruction).

But every day brings a new visitor
and another attempt at the quintessential cup.
Now Gretchen's brought
Celestial Seasonings Variety Pack
and a Honey Bear
(all my guests agree
there's a Honey Bear in every lesbian home.
That's how they knew the nurse they'd been cruising
wasn't one of us after all.
She thought it was syrup.)
Inspira and Ahavia, Fai and Laura
leave their thermoses.
Home from the hospital
trapped on the second floor

where the kitchen is only a distant memory
I line up all the supplies on my bedside table
wait for today's company to arrive
and reason that even a hardcore stomping diesel dyke
can't ruin a pot of boiling water
can she?

Covered

The first night home from the hospital
I couldn't sleep
I was so cold
I asked for blankets and my friends
came through.
Yours is woven wool
Gordon plaid: forest green and indigo
with a small white rectangle
marked "Freeport, Maine."
It's sandwiched between
two fuzzy layers of
benign baby blue.

You ask to borrow my sleeping bag.
You are about to go traveling
in New England
with your lover
it's early October and
you want to sleep outside.
We make the exchange. You search
my closet, and shove the bright
unwieldy genie
into the pudgy stuff sack
tie it on your back
to bicycle crosstown home.

I wake at five a.m.
in pain, but finally
warm enough.
My friends have left me
a thermos of hot Sleepytime tea.
I turn back a flap

of covers for a corner
of your clear, even plaid
a serene sail
a fresh imprint on my
gently breaking
morning.

Spells of Blindness

(for my roommate in Vermont—January, 1983)

You tell me these spells of blindness
are recurring, periodic
you can't predict when one will come
or how long it will last.
So you count steps
learn to open locks by touch
arrange your possessions carefully
in the compartments of any strange
new space.

You won't talk about
how these hours frighten you
and when I ask what causes them
fall silent

I can guess.
When you tell of your life
you skim past
beatings, broken bones.
Your years on the street were brief
but you paid for them
with your innocence
half your hearing
four babies lost and now
little by little
your sight.
I don't know what
internal injuries
you've sustained
what's hidden under that
streetwise act, that crusted
scar tissue.

You've been emerging
from that life

taking chances.
You want to write, turn
what has hurt you
into words. You tell me
you want to fall in love.
I listen
with fingers crossed
willing you not to collide, not to fall
not to suffer another single blow

And you must face this:
doctors agree
these spells will grow in
frequency, in length
as you grow older.
The doctors have run tests:
they are positive.

I long to take you by the hand
and guide you gently through
a safe, peaceful life

I stand aside
and let your fingers find
the wall, the door,
explore your light-proof world.
I twist my own fingers
together
and don't talk about
how this frightens me,
only repeat

what I long to believe, what
I long for you to live:

That damage to the nerve
may result in loss of sight
but you will never
let it
lead to
total loss of vision.

Two Poems for the Woman Who Has Everything

RSVP

Our lives ran parallel
        both of us poets
        close in years
        women who love women.
Everything I wanted
        you got.

Of course, you were blond
        with a head full of curls
        nice new clothes every year
        younger than I
yet I knew I was pretty, too
        bright and wise
        full of generosity
and I wanted the hearth to come home to
        the houseful of children
        the whole blossoming garden.

But it was you who got
        the companion who is with you still
        eleven years later.
You got the house that
        "felt like falling in love
        all over again"
the same year
        my lover came home to every new
        plumbing and heating disaster
        slamming doors and screaming
        "I hate this house!"

You opened your hands and things came into them
        the lines of poetry I wished I had written
        work that you love

and money to pay you for it—
enough for all the things you want in your life.
You got the baby who came
        with his own name
        and chose the two of you.

Nothing comes to me without a struggle—
        my hard-won friends
        this frugal, simple life
        my tenuous notoriety
        shaky sense of self
        my art.
Everything demands
        continual watchful tending.
To everything
        I must be constantly feeding fuel.
Everything
        is always in need of repair.

I know you are not responsible
        for this imbalance.
I present it only as explanation
        for my regrets.
I cannot come to your open home
        enjoy your company
        join in your celebration of
        another year fulfilled—

I'm sorry.
I cannot attend the party.

COUNTERWEIGHTS

You with your lover
your long years behind you
before you
your house with more rooms than
you knew what to do with
hearths upstairs and down
multiple flights of fancy
and out the garden door so long
a length of green—

You bring poems about
raising Baby. You win
the fertility lottery, get
pregnant with a second child. I get
to go out at night. I win
prizes, get published. I write
about wanting a baby.

We're set in motion by
this counterbalance
between us we never
speak of, rocking
one side up
the other down like two
unmatched swings in a
playground, a nursery boat
an empty cradle.

Yet there was something you wanted
still:
When I finally found my home alone
and first showed it to everyone

trooping up the single stairs
creaking the floorboards
crowding doorways
in and out of the few
plain, small rooms,
something you saw made you
pause in the hall
at the top of the narrow descent
look back over your shoulder to my
bare room with bed made
ready for simple sleep.

You only said, "This is really
a sweet little house,"
but I heard
that wistfulness under your tongue
I saw
even in the dark
that lingering
longing.

The Way I Want to Be Friends

*(with thanks to Susan Windle for her
"Work Poem" which inspired this)*

Can we touch each other more, please?
Can we each have our fill of hugs every day,
fill each other's arms again and again

Can we let our bare arms brush against each other's
and our knees bump, with no apologies
squeeze close together in small spaces
can we tickle and tumble and remember play
giggle and stop with a head plopped in an open lap

Can we braid each other's hair
sprinkle each other's feet
spread each other's backs with pungent oils
slip the rings from finger to finger
fasten the clasp at the neck's nape
wrap each other's heads in wide, woven bands

Can we spend the day together
laugh and lean against one another
catch hands in the sunlight and leave them linked
and swinging in the rhythm of our matching stride

Can we spend the night together
and not end up ex-lovers
can we cuddle close on a blanket under stars
and tell each other stories, sing each other songs
lie long in one another's arms
holding, holding through the dark

Can we touch each other more please
can we fill each other's lives
can we fill each other
again and again and again?

My Vision of a Women's Community

I call my friend to find out if she owns
a round cake pan
deep dish
"the kind with the hole in the middle?"

Yes— but she's on her way out the door.
She'll leave it on the porch.
the four blocks between our houses
vibrate with color from every garden
all blossoms wide open
so early in the day.

Up the stairs, on the porch
the cake pan waits in a corner.
The downstairs neighbor's mother
who speaks no English
nods and smiles at me.

I bake a cake with cinnamon and sour cream
from a recipe passed on to me,
invert it on my prettiest plate
to take to the potluck.

My friend is there, too
with chips and pasta salad.
I've remembered to bring her cake pan
but she says I can keep it—

she hardly ever makes that kind of
cake any more
but if she wants to
she can always borrow it back.

"Anytime—"
She already has the keys to my house.
Like everyone else, she loves the cake
and probably will never know
that in this simple back and forth
this day-long thread of gifts
I've been given
something I've wanted all my life.

COMING TO TERMS WITH MYSELF

Coming to Terms with Myself

(for my writing group with gratitude and humility)

Can you believe this?
Here's this woman
articulate, intelligent
with a bachelor's degree
and a Master of Fine Arts in Creative Writing—
She won third prize in the
Celebrate Food in Poetry Contest
a Pennsylvania Fellowship the year before
and now she's just been awarded a grant
from the National Endowment for the Arts
which will support her for a year
while she does nothing but write.

She's personal friends with feminist editors
all over the place.
She's got people asking her to do workshops
from Los Angeles, California to Bloomington, Indiana
reviews coming in from the San Francisco Chronicle
and the Mama Bears News
publishers waiting to hear from her
in England and Denmark.
She's given eighty-seven public readings of
her own original work
which has been published in ten anthologies
and twenty-nine periodicals
not to mention her own two books.
I mean, she's hot.

She's also just written this new poem
and she's bringing it to a meeting
and handing out xeroxed copies to
a group who might appear to be
perfectly ordinary women
some of whom have never been published anywhere
except that

she's biting her fingers
examining the floor.
Her ears are bright red and she's
trying to stop her knees from shaking
because she wants to know your opinion,
I mean, whether she's
really a writer
or has only been faking it
all these years.
No, seriously,
is this a poem
or isn't it?
Come on gang—
I'm depending on you.

8 Reasons Why You Will Never Make It
   in the Corporate World

1. Let's start with the shoes. They'll never do. Too flat.
   Too plain. Too dull— nobody would ever notice the
   ankles or the legs. Besides, they don't match anything
   else you're wearing.

2. That stuff your blouses are made out of isn't right. It
   doesn't fall correctly, has no sparkle. It doesn't do
   anything for your figure. Anyway, the necklines are all
   too high. And didn't you already wear that one last week?

3. Pants?

4. The hands won't do: those short, stubby, unenameled nails.
   The skin's too dry— all paper cuts and calluses. What
   do you do when you're not working, wash dishes and scrub
   floors?

5. That face. It just isn't enough, all by itself. It needs
   more color in the lips, the cheeks, a little mystery about
   the eyes. Let's not even discuss the eyebrows and those—
   wisps around the chin.

6. Haven't you tried to do anything with your hair?

7. There ought to be accessories— a thin gold chain, or
   maybe pearls. Earrings, an attractive watch. An
   unobtrusive leather purse, swinging from one shoulder or
   clutched under an arm. . . .

8. In conclusion: You're all wrong. We just can't ignore the
   final, overall effect. You're not a man.

For Those Who Suffer from Chronic Mismanagement of Their Own Time

Leave work one half hour early.
Think of all you could be doing to fill up
    this small treasure of open time.
On a large sheet of paper
make a list of every one of those things you know
    you ought to be doing
or rather, make a chart.
Write upside down, along the edges and in corners.
Draw detailed diagrams with step by step instructions.
Include intricate illustrations, underlining,
    and exclamation points!
Don't stop
    until every square inch of space is full.
Make it as demanding, as imposing,
    as impossible as you like.

Make it as demanding,
    and imposing
    and impossible as your life.
Read it over and take it all in.
Next, crease the chart evenly into a fold
    along one edge.
Turn it over and fold again.
Continue until you have pleated the entire surface
    into a paper fan.
All the words and diagrams will make
    interesting designs along the edges and will be
    completely illegible.
Fan in hand,
stretch out full length in a comfortable spot.
Gently fan yourself to sleep.

Savings & Loan

The teller at the bank calls out
"Can I help who's next?"
And the man at the head of the line
answers loudly
"Yes! You can! It's me— I'm next."
All heads turn to find out who
this eccentric character is.
Mine, too.

I find it's an old lover
in a London Fog trenchcoat,
leather briefcase at his side.
Flamboyantly, he sweeps to place
before the window grill.
I watch until
my watching turns his head—
his face lights up.
Mine, too.

We slept together on a box spring
the summer I first left home
surrounded by dirty shirts on chair backs
piles of books on the floor
next to the hot plate, his portable typewriter
set up for another act of his endless play.
Three other rugged individuals
shared his two room hospitality.
Mine, too.

Eighteen years later now
it no longer matters
that he once called me his concubine.
We smile at one another

across the velvet loops that demarcate the line.
His delight in who he has become is obvious.
In who I have remained,
mine, too.

I find myself forgiving
those mistaken months, misunderstanding years,
find, to my surprise, this
forgiveness is not only his but
mine, too. I'm ready to
forgive myself for loving him.
It's time. I'm first in line.

My Next Lover

My next lover will have a car
maybe a Mercedes.
She won't expect me to bicycle
anywhere!

If we're going to a family wedding
an awards dinner or
a program in the black community on a
Sunday afternoon
where I'm the keynote speaker—
she'll wear a skirt.

My next lover will love kids.
She might even have one or two
of her own. In any case
she'll be crazy about mine.
She'll be thrilled to babysit
when I have to go out of town
even if it's for a month.

My next lover will have something she's
impassioned about and obsessed with
besides me.
There'll be times when she can't wait to
get back to whatever she's
creating. There'll be whole weekends
when she doesn't care

what I do, and won't even notice
if we haven't made love.

But my next lover will always be
available for me.
Whenever I'm ready
her timing will be perfect.

My next lover will be wild about
communication.
When I ask her what's wrong
she'll come out with more than
two syllables.

My next lover will never give up on us.
She'll believe in couples therapy.
If we reach a point where the whole thing
just isn't working anymore—
she'll change.

My next lover can flirt with whomever she likes.
We'll both know it's not serious.
And while many women will probably want her
my next lover will want to stay with me.
She'll know she'll never get
a better offer.

Plumstone

eating a plum
I tongue the tight skin
drawn seam
that halves this globed
whole in two
it's midnight
blue outside
but when I bite in
bursting
with wet red flesh
the juice dripping down
my fingers sweet
sticky sticky
sweet pulp
engorged I
fill my mouth
eat it down
eat it down
all the way to the
plumstone.

Finding Myself Still Here at Thirty-Seven

This is who I am
in the vacant lot down at the corner
face tipped skyward, arm stretched high to
pull down a branch of the mulberry tree

dropping berries into my pail. Strays
roll down inside the bib of my overalls
and make me laugh.

This is who
I have always been an
original. Perennial.

In the kitchen I beat up batter for muffins
tumble the berries in
I make yoghurt, I make a
sharp cheese and onion quiche
from a recipe that nobody likes but me

Next morning the mulberry muffins taste
sweet but mostly wild
the taste lingers on my tongue

I walk to my job in a high rise
office building downtown
wearing stockings
wearing a skirt
with mulberry juice stains under my fingernails.

For the Old Country

Coming from a reading in the northwest end of town
    we drive through my old neighborhood
      pass the playground where I played as a child
I show you my old school
then direct you down
West Duval Street
    slow now,
        slower,
           stop
               in the middle of the block
That's the one: Fifty-two
    the last in that red brick row.
My family sold it twenty years ago
    but I can't let go of
    this place I can never come home to

I stare and stare out the window of the car
I see
    small houses, squat and low
    strung one to another like
    square nursery beads
    this one— with a wrought iron gate
      a scrap of yard and a tree
    plain but well kept and cared for
    like all the others on this honest block
    where hardworking folk come home to be families
      cook their pork and greens
      sweep clean front steps
      call and call their children in
      and rest on these porches at summers days' ends

But I wonder what you see
you who have been
    all your life

a refugee
born to a people acceptable to hate and despise,
across an ocean to this cradle
    come, already half-grown
you for whom no language is home
    no birthright
    no safety assured
    no guarantee unconditional
whose childhood held no time for play
    no reason for laughter
the riverbanks you wandered alone
    long left behind
streets from which someone called you home
    long ago destroyed

You offer a handful of wistful words:
    the places where we lived— so many
        no longer exist
    I would not know how to find them if they did
    I would not know how to begin.

There is something the rest of us keep letting happen
        over and over again

        Isei, Nisei
        Chicana, Riqueño
        Cherokee
        Haitian, Cuban
        Hmong
        Ashkenazi, Sephardi
        Arab and Ethiopian

Migrant Worker
Exile
Undesireable Alien

Victim of the Dustbowl
Diaspora
Holocaust
The Middle Passage
The Trail of Tears

Displaced/ resettled/ uprooted/ removed
What does this quiet neighborhood mean
 to you?
Oblivious, I chant facts
as if my words could make it mine again
 I used to swing on that gate
 my father made the picket fence
 we had blue awnings on the porch
I point and say I planted that maple tree
 by that fence
 when I was a little girl
What can it mean to you for whom
 home is not even a place
 you can stop
 and stand outside of
 longing?

There Are No Trees in China

—There are no trees in China—
Elsa says. She has just returned.
We sit
at the top of Bald Hill
look out across a valley to
another forested mountainside.

—There are no trees in China
no wilderness.
All of the land is either crops or homes,
at least, in the parts of China I was shown.

There are— she says— no houseflies in China.
Some years ago, there was a great campaign
in which
the houseflies all were killed—

But I have heard
there are no rich in China
no bosses over factories
no exploitation of women's bodies, as here
no drug abuse, addiction
all of the people wear pants
quilted jackets
and sensible cotton shoes

—Yes— she says— yes, but
there are no birds in China.
They ate the crops.
The people didn't want them.
Just as it was
with the houseflies—

Around us there is green
in every direction

the thick tall grasses
the wooded mountainside

and surely some subtle balance
would be
upset
by the absence of small birds.

I remember I have read:
There are no homosexuals in China.
It was written with pride.
It was only one of many
problems that had been solved.

Race Point Light

I walked to the lighthouse at Race Point Beach.
The tide was out
the marshes green as fire
against incessant blue.

Mid-afternoon I reached it.
Three gulls perched
on the ridge of a house.
The house was boarded up.

The tower was metal
seamed and welded like a ship.
I walked the whole way round.
The door was locked.

I had always thought that someone kept the light
some kindly old man—
whiskered,
white
lit the beacon here when night began to fall.

There is only the cold beam
gleaming
revolving ceaselessly in the stark broad light of day
sweeping the land
the sea,
indifferent

And no one else but me.

A Father Hits His Two Children

A father hits his two children.
One child takes it in stride
the other takes it in
permanently.
In school she cries easily, constantly.
She cannot make mistakes.
She cannot ask for help.

A father punishes his children.
One of them is grateful to him for
finally spanking some sense into her
the other stays scarred.
Twenty-five years later
she cannot get angry at anyone
feels she must always please
she feels that nothing she does is ever
good enough
she doesn't deserve to be loved.

A father disciplines his two children.
He turns them over his knee.
He smacks with his hand.
He uses the back of a hairbrush.
He takes off his belt and strikes with it.
He slices switches from the hedge
and switches legs until they sting.
He is always bigger, stronger, louder
than everyone else in the house.

A father hits his two daughters.
One of them tells her mother about it
twenty-five years later
trying to explain why she is

still afraid of her father.
The mother seems surprised,
calls in the older daughter to
confirm the story.

The older daughter says
He didn't.
Anyway, she says
He didn't do it much.
Anyway, she says
He didn't spank us any more
than anyone else's father spanked them.
She says
That wasn't abuse.

The mother asks
Where was I when this was going on?
The younger daughter feels a wild leap
of hope in her chest.
Her mother never knew!
Surely she will be angry
and on her side.
The mother says
I would have been there
if that had been going on
I would remember.
I don't remember anything like that.
It couldn't have happened.

A father hits his two daughters.
Twenty-five years later
he has never said he is sorry.
The older daughter

never thought he needed to.
She always knew that he loved
them both.
The younger daughter
remembers.

Love Poem to Anger
            an incantation

May there be space for anger in my home
May anger be always welcome to pass through

Let me keep a hearth for anger
and learn to use it like fire

Let my life be like a basin
which anger fills
and from which anger drains

Let my body be an instrument
a chamber where anger resonates
Let my throat be a channel
through which anger is sounded
and released

Let me be attuned to anger's presence
sense when anger is at home
like a familiar companion
whose ways I know
and trust

Let me listen for anger's voice
beneath the sweetness or the tears
muffled under the sadness, the hunger,
the need to sleep

Let me come to know anger's face
to meet that gaze
and no longer be afraid of it

Let me open myself to anger's touch
to be shaken through to my fingertips
charged with purpose

with that fierce, protective power
Let me learn to recognize whose touch this is
and that it cannot hurt me

May I keep anger pure, in its own form
and not dilute it
and not disguise it
and not transform it into anything
more easily accepted

May anger be accepted for itself, in my home
May I claim my own anger for my own
May I receive it as a gift
May I let anger teach me
May I follow where anger leads me

Let me love myself angry!

Now I open the door to anger.
Now I open the windows to anger.
Now I open the walls to anger.
Now I open the heart.

Love Poem to Myself

(for my fortieth birthday)

Happy Birthday whoever you are
little one
old one
love of my life
my likeness
my most cherished darkness
my radiance

innocent
knowing one
with the wide eyes
open hands
wide open heart
I open
my heart to you.

Listen—
I will be exactly who you need:
wise mother
all forgiving lover
playful sister
listening, intimate friend

I will love you no matter what.
I will love you at any cost.
I will love you the way
you deserve to be loved.
Nothing you could do
could keep me from loving you.
This is my gift for you
this year this day this hour
for you whom I love most of all

You may get whatever you want to get.
You may have whatever you want to have.

You may feel whatever it is you feel.
You may do whatever you want to do
most of all
You may be who you
always were
always will be
who you
absolutely amazingly
all ways
already are.

About the Author

Becky Birtha is the author of two collections of short stories, *For Nights Like this One: Stories of Loving Women* (Frog in the Well, 1983) and *Lovers' Choice* (Seal, 1987). She received an Individual Fellowship in Literature from the Pennsylvania Council on the Arts in 1985, and a Creative Writing Fellowship Grant from the National Endowment for the Arts in 1988. A black lesbian feminist Quaker in the process of becoming a mother, she wrote many of these poems throughout recovering from the loss of a long-time relationship. *The Forbidden Poems* is her first published book of poetry.

Selected Titles from Seal Press

Lovers' Choice by Becky Birtha. $8.95, 0-931188-56-3. Stories that chart the course of black women's lives and relationships.

Nervous Conditions by Tsitsi Dangarembga. $8.95, 0-931188-74-1. A moving story of a Zimbabwean girl's coming of age and a compelling narrative of the devastating human loss involved in the colonization of one culture by another.

Angel by Merle Collins. $8.95 0-931188-64-4. This novel from Grenada follows young Angel McAllister as she joins her country's move toward political autonomy.

Miss Venezuela by Barbara Wilson. $9.95, 0-931188-58-X. A provocative collection of twenty-two new and previously published stories by a well-known lesbian author.

Voyages Out 2: Lesbian Short Fiction by Julie Blackwomon and Nona Caspers. $8.95, 0-931188-90-3. In this second volume of our series designed to showcase talented short fiction writers, two fresh voices report on lesbian life in distinctive ways.

The Things That Divide Us edited by Faith Conlon, Rachel da Silva and Barbara Wilson. $8.95, 0-931188-32-6. Sixteen stories exploring issues of racism, anti-Semitism and class difference by many of today's top feminist writers.

The Black Women's Health Book: Speaking for Ourselves edited by Evelyn C. White. $14.95, 0-931188-86-5. Each of the forty-one contributions in this pioneering anthology testifies to the determination of black women to get well and stay well. Contributors include Faye Wattleton, Byllye Avery, Alice Walker and Angela Y. Davis.

Chain Chain Change: For Black Women Dealing With Physical and Emotional Abuse by Evelyn C. White. $5.95, 0-931188-25-3. The first book on domestic violence as it is experienced, interpreted and challenged by black women.

Ceremonies of the Heart: Celebrating Lesbian Unions edited by Becky Butler. $14.95, 0-931188-92-X. A celebration of love and lesbian pride, this anthology takes you into the lives of twenty-seven couples who have affirmed their relationships with rituals—weddings, handfastings, holy unions and ceremonies of commitment.

Seal Press, founded in 1976 to publish women writers, has many other titles in stock: fiction, self-help books, anthologies and international literature. Any of the books above may be ordered from us at 3131 Western Avenue, Suite 410, Seattle, WA 98121 (include $2.00 for the first book and .50 for each additional book). Write to us for a free catalog or if you would like to be on our mailing list.

1764